Other 'crazy' gigglebooks by Bill Stott
Sex – it drives us crazy!
Marriage – it drives us crazy!
Football – it drives us crazy!
Rugby – it drives us crazy!

Published simultaneously in 2004 by Helen Exley Giftbooks in Great Britain, and Helen Exley Giftbooks LLC in the USA

12 11 10 9 8 7 6 5 4 3

Selection and arrangement copyright © 2004 Helen Exley
Cartoons copyright © 2004 Bill Stott
Design by 451° <studio@451.uk.com>

ISBN 1-86187-754-4

Printed in China

Helen Exley Giftbooks, 16 Chalk Hill, Watford, Herts, WD19 4BG, UK
Helen Exley Giftbooks, 185 Main Street, Spencer MA 01562, USA
www.helenexleygiftbooks.com

A HELEN EXLEY
GIGGLEBOOK

Cats

THEY DRIVE US CRAZY!

CARTOONS BY BILL STOTT

40p

"I think that hairdryer
is too powerful for him..."

"A whole 25lb turkey? Nonsense.
No cat could eat a whole 25lb turkey."

"All that stuff about bringing them gifts – it's rubbish. We do it just to scare them!"

"Oh, come, come – does she look like a cat who'd make a smell?"

"How come I get thrown out when the flea was found on the carpet?"

"Well, of course she's growling. You put ketchup on your steak, and she hates ketchup!"

"Since she stayed at the Hilton,
she's become so fastidious..."

"And when she actually
deigns to come home,
we'll do our tiger ambush!"

1

"Uh-oh – he knows it's cheap soya substitute."

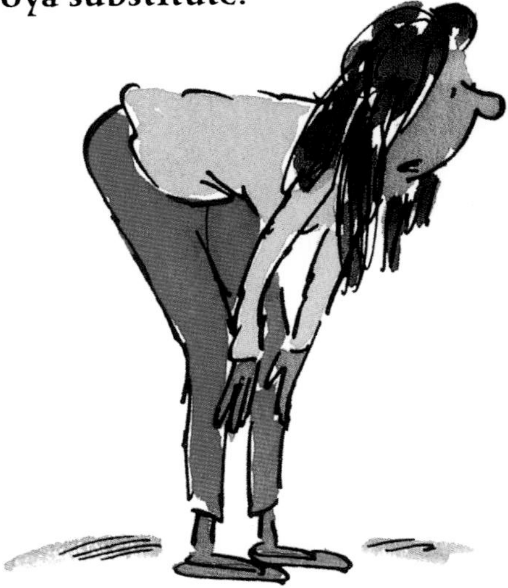

"Play with the yarn. Don't kill it!"

"They do say that cats know what you're thinking."

"Normally I'd have to admit you're a pretty humdrum kind of guy. But with that can-opener in your hand, you're a giant."

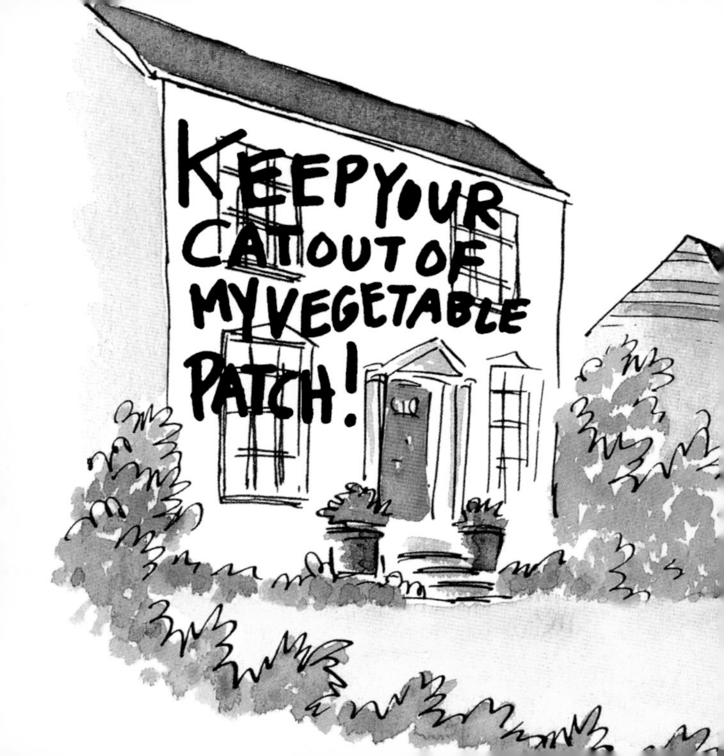
KEEP YOUR CAT OUT OF MY VEGETABLE PATCH!

"Satisfy my curiosity – if you could
get at me, would you actually eat me?"

1

"A simple `yes` or `no` will do."

"I'll wait until someone comes by before
I go and have a drink. I just love those
cries of middle-class outrage."

About Bill Stott

Bill Stott is a freelance cartoonist whose work never fails to pinpoint the absurd and simply daft moments in our daily lives. Originally Head of Arts faculty at a city high school, Bill launched himself as a freelance cartoonist in 1976. With sales of 2.8 million books with Helen Exley Giftbooks, Bill has an impressive portfolio of 26 published titles, including his very successful *Spread of Over 40's Jokes* and *Triumph of Over 50's Jokes*.

Bill's work appears in many publications and magazines, ranging from the *The Times Educational Supplement* to *Practical Poultry*. An acclaimed after-dinner speaker, Bill subjects his audience to a generous helping of his wit and wisdom, illustrated with cartoons drawn deftly on the spot!

What is a Helen Exley giftbook?

We hope you enjoy *Cats – they drive us crazy!*. It's just one of many hilarious cartoon books available from Helen Exley Giftbooks, all of which make special gifts. We try our best to bring you the funniest jokes because we want every book we publish to be great to give, great to receive.

HELEN EXLEY GIFTBOOKS creates gifts for all special occasions – not just birthdays, anniversaries, weddings and Christmas, but for those times when you just want to say 'thanks' or 'I love you'. Why not visit our website, www. helenexleygiftbooks.com, and browse through all our present ideas?

ALSO BY BILL STOTT
Marriage – it drives us crazy!
Football – it drives us crazy!
Rugby – it drives us crazy!
Sex – it drives us crazy!

Information on all our titles is also available from
Helen Exley Giftbooks, 16 Chalk Hill, Watford WD19 4BG, UK. Tel 01923 250505
Helen Exley Giftbooks, 185 Main Street, Spencer MA 01562, USA. Tel 877 395 3942